Animals That Live in the Grasslands

Ostriches

Therese Harasymiw

3 1336 08716 8853

Gareth Stevens
Publishing

Please visit our Web site, www.garethstevens.com. For a free color catalog of all our high-quality books, call toll free 1-800-542-2595 or fax 1-877-542-2596.

Library of Congress Cataloging-in-Publication Data

Harasymiw, Therese.
Ostriches / Therese Harasymiw.
   p. cm. – (Animals that live in the grasslands)
Includes index.
ISBN 978-1-4339-3879-5 (pbk.)
ISBN 978-1-4339-3880-1 (6-pack)
ISBN 978-1-4339-3878-8 (library binding)
1. Ostriches—Juvenile literature. I. Title.
QL696.S9H37 2010
598.5'24—dc22
                                                    2010013452

First Edition

Published in 2011 by
Gareth Stevens Publishing
111 East 14th Street, Suite 349
New York, NY 10003

Designer: Michael J. Flynn
Editor: Therese Shea

Photo credits: Cover, pp. 1, 5, 7, 11, 13, 15, 17, 19, 21, back cover Shutterstock.com; p. 9 Simon Maina/AFP/Getty Images.

Printed in the United States of America

CPSIA compliance information: Batch #CS10GS: For further information contact Gareth Stevens, New York, New York at 1-800-542-2595.

Table of Contents

Boldface words appear in the glossary.

Biggest Bird of All

Have you ever seen a bird taller than you? Ostriches are the tallest birds in the world.

They live in the **grasslands** and deserts of Africa.

5

Wings and Legs

Ostriches have short wings. They can't fly. Their long legs help them get around. When an ostrich runs, each step may cover 16 feet (4.9 m)!

long legs

short wings

7

Ostriches can run up to 43 miles (69 km) per hour. That's as fast as a car!

Some people ride ostriches in races.

Ostriches also use their long, powerful legs as **weapons.** An ostrich's kick can kill a lion! Each foot has long, sharp claws.

claws

Male ostriches have black and white feathers. **Females** have grey and brown feathers. Males use their wings to show off! They shake and wave their wings at females.

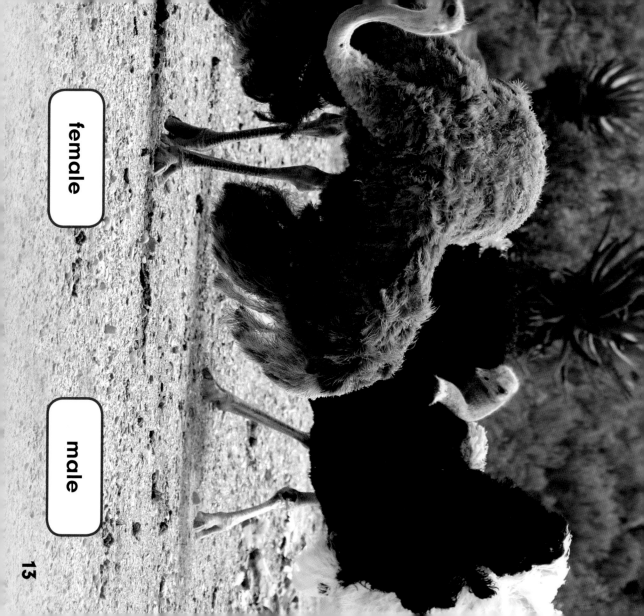

female

male

13

Herds of Birds

Ostriches live in herds. They bend their heads to eat.

Usually one ostrich can spot enemies while others eat.

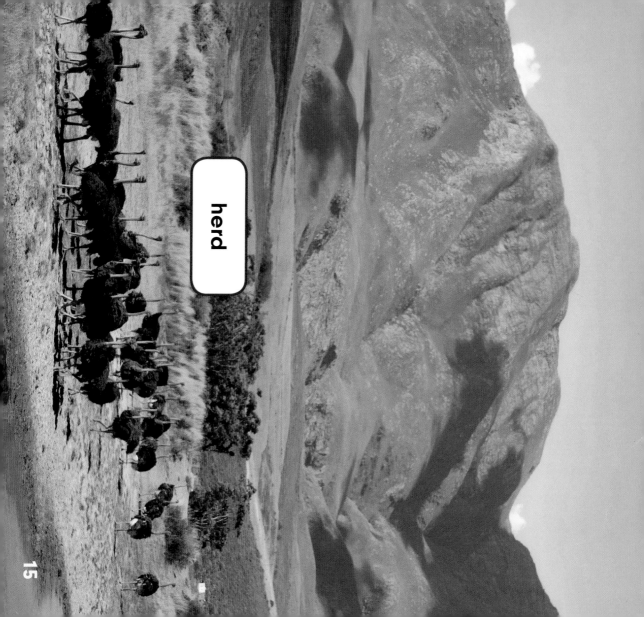

herd

Ostriches eat roots, leaves, seeds, bugs, and lizards. They also eat sand and stones! These help break up food in their stomach.

All the females in a herd put their eggs into one nest. One ostrich egg is as heavy as 24 chicken eggs!

ostrich
egg

chicken
egg

The herd's top male and top female take turns sitting on the nest. They use their wings to cover the nest. The eggs **hatch** after about 45 days.

Fast Facts

Height	up to 9 feet (2.7 meters)
Weight	up to 350 pounds (160 kilograms)
Egg	length: 6 by 5 inches (15 by 13 centimeters) weight: about 3 pounds (1,360 grams)
Diet	roots, leaves, seeds, bugs, lizards, and other plants and animals; sand and stones
Average life span	up to 40 years in the wild

Glossary

female: a girl

grasslands: land on which grass is the main kind of plant life

hatch: to come out of an egg

male: a boy

weapon: a tool used to hurt an animal or a person

For More Information

Books

Lunis, Natalie. *Ostrich: The World's Biggest Bird*. New York, NY: Bearport Publishing, 2007.

Maynard, Thane. *Ostriches*. Chanhassen, MN: Child's World, 2007.

Web Sites

Birds: Ostrich
www.sandiegozoo.org/animalbytes/t-ostrich.html
Read about ostriches, and see photos of an ostrich nest and babies.

Ostriches
kids.nationalgeographic.com/Animals/ CreatureFeature/Ostrich
Read more about an ostrich's life in the grasslands.

Publisher's note to educators and parents: Our editors have carefully reviewed these Web sites to ensure that they are suitable for students. Many Web sites change frequently, however, and we cannot guarantee that a site's future contents will continue to meet our high standards of quality and educational value. Be advised that students should be closely supervised whenever they access the Internet.

Index

About the Author

Therese Harasymiw spent many summers of her youth working on an ostrich ranch. Today, she is a writer and editor in Buffalo, New York.